BOTTLE

Ramona Herdman

HAPPENSTANCE

By the same author:
Come What You Wished For, Egg Box, 2003

Printed by The Dolphin Press
www.dolphinpress.co.uk

First published in 2017 by HappenStance Press,
21 Hatton Green, Glenrothes, Fife KY7 4SD
nell@happenstancepress.com
www.happenstancepress.com

CONTENTS

SHIP IN A BOTTLE

You hope it's like a genie but it's more like a ship.
What's in this bottle is amazing as a ship's folded rigging,
as her nine sheets stowed neat (but longing to throw

themselves to the wind, flapping sting-wet rope-ends).
Amazing, how she sails from the liquid's doldrums—
a single, some doubles, straight from the bottle.

Amazing how she changes you—you're almost
still the person peering at this from outside, saying
Just one, but the deck flexes under your feet

and you're back on your sea-legs, face burnt, lips cracked
with the years since you last saw land. Amazing how quick
she turns and you stagger. She flies in front of the wind,

sails laughing, full rig, every creak and crack of her
saying this is what she was made for. And you,
borne along like a whole crew, singing.

I TELL THE STORY LIKE GRACE

and again then
liquid's hush
stumble of ice cubes
glass misting in shock

again then
a shot on the rocks
a taste to train yourself into
following father's fathers

every time slicing lemon
selecting glasses
I need to tell
the family temptation

keeping an eye
on the old yellow devil
making the ghost exist
again a storm from a bottle

I take the glass
its kit of spirit
ticking ice
garnish

wish for a hand
gently squeezing my brain
a small fire licking
a spell in a glass

YES

Boy at the off licence,
you are slightly too old for this job
and you are not beautiful.

But you hold my eye

so I say *Yes*
to the taster of pink fizz

refused by the sensible women
(*working   driving   kids*)
ahead of me in the queue.

It is 11 am on Sunday
and you look like you know
the way out of the weight of the world.

So yes, I will run away with you

at least as far
as the bins round the back
with the rest of the bottle.

SHE'S NOT HERSELF

It is her illness makes her like this—
first kiss instant, readily bedded,
radiant. Then off for a month

with another. Not her fault—
it is the illness makes her
tornado and tornadoed.

If there were a day she was well
you could judge if it's her or the illness
that ignores your texts, makes promises.

As it is, she's almost always chasing
the instant's enthusiasm—tonight sex, tomorrow yoga,
next week long distance running, the tango and anorexia.

The illness dumps her in bed
on the off days, she says, like a flatbed truck
tipping gravel. Other days,

the illness spins you up into her atmosphere.
Take her hand and see the stars
gather round her head like midges.

Then she drops you
           back in the world with the others,
same as you ever were,
           for a wonder.

FIRST DRINK OF THE NIGHT

Reliable magic. Undimmed spring.
Peter Pan at the window, laughing,
reaching his hand in, lifting you
light on the empty air, the horizon
opening up like the sea arriving.

THE INHERITED DRINK

Half seven, the day ahead,
and my true thought is that a drink
would make it better—just a nip
to deaden it.

My dead father grins. He's proud.
He shakes his head, *You get that from me.*

A little less reality—
penumbra of fuzz, three second
delay. I don't want to touch it.

DRINKING PARTNER

You would sit in the kitchen, drinking alone
every night of my childhood. Cheap whisky. Joints.
You cleared up after yourself. You went to work
before we woke up.

I shouldn't have been so young so long and you—
you shouldn't be so dead. Perhaps we could haunt
each other, bring our nights together, now I've
grown my drinking legs.

One night I'll walk in on you in that kitchen.
We'll knock it back like medicine. No talking.
Or you're welcome at mine, any night. I've a
quiver of whiskies.

You are the person I'd like most to drink with.
I leave a glass of Bells out at night—like kids,
I hope, still do for Father Christmas. It makes
the morning smell of you.

FROM 'THE DRUNK CIRCUS'

1. Trapeze artists

O acrobats
is glorious

the letting go you do
enough for all of us.

Your derring-do
across the air.

the arc of you
Your catch and hook.

The high trapeze.
on with your knees

The way you hold
your teeth,

your very edges.
The spun-steel gaze

The run up.
across the abyss.

The two of you
drink each other up

matching shot for shot,
to the heavens.

Beyond our
breath,

earthbound
you trust

you hold each other
with your berserk

up
belief.

2. Trick rider

She loves the white horse. She loves
the damage it could do her.

Six stone, she tiptoes, reaches
to attach the spangled pommel.

She loves scaring her audience.
She loves the skill, tilt at full gallop.

Every night flying in circles
out of her skull. Faster and faster.

3. Freaks

Some towns, the circus beds down with a fair—
the hucksters, the cheats, the waltzers.
The freakshow's stalls like any Friday night main drag—
the woman bearded with vomit,
the high-heeled twins conjoined
by love and stagger, the man
who coats himself in bees, or bangs nails
through his tender, leaping skin,
or takes any man's punch
to his belly, that man who lives by his hurt.

MY FATHER'S COUGH

My teenage mornings, my father coughing
round the house. Maddening. Like roadworks,
explosions in a jam jar, a printer
resetting itself over and over.
I wanted to reach through his ribs
and pull out the bloody trouble, treacle
mucus, needling irritant, whatever. Every day.

Decades later, with bronchitis,
I shuffle and hack round the house. I spit
slugs in the shower. I cough blood. I've no
patience with it: I want to cough my heart up.
I want to get to the bit where I find him
on the garden bench, tea steaming in weak sun,
the first fag of the day settling his chest.

PRODIGAL

O beautiful arsewipe, improvident prodigal,
swagger back and we'll all be fall-down grateful.
There are more than enough of us being sensible.
We need a bit of outrage, a fuck-it-all ne'er do well.

Let's learn again together how it always ends.
O shockingly less-lovely, look again
at me with those two-bit trading-bead eyes, sing
for your succour as you always did, ruin.

IN VINO

The wurm that I am
put its blind head out to bite

last night, all sweaty roils,
snigger and whimper and spite.

I wasn't sure I was so small
and sneaking until today

when you told me that I'd said
the opposite of what I always say.

I would have thought I couldn't think that
but there's no denying where

the wurm lives—who is its foul
source, its spoilheap nest of hair.

THE DRINK IS NOT THE PROBLEM

If you could see your own problem
you'd know it couldn't be so.

Without the drink,
the problem marauds.

The problems the drink brings
are diversions from the problem.

The problem lives in a well
and the drink keeps it down there.

'MY NAME IS LEGION: FOR WE ARE MANY'
—Mark 5:1-20

My favourite miracle—the casting out
of devils from the cut and howling man
who lived in tombs above the town.

It cast them into swine, a panicking that sped
the herd to drown themselves like lightning
in the sea. I feel for the townspeople,

the lawful, who thought the madman unbearable trouble
until they saw the miracle—and then
begged the saint (on their knees) to go, godspeed,

even gave him a boat.
            Then had to eat the pork,
fished out, boiled down to brawn, for lack.

Had to watch each other, in fear,
for symptoms of contagion.
I think of them when I visit your stink.

When I reach in, bare-armed, to pull you from your bed.
When I suggest sunlight. When clearing up.
When I talk in a voice even I hate, of hope.

PICNIC

She packed for romance: a feast
      in wicker, bitters for gin. Wore ringlets
and her thank you knickers.

      And though there were earwigs
and fingers squirming
      like something from inside a crab

and juice from the blackberries
      forever staining the gingham,
she had no complaints.

      There was sun, partly,
and she taught him
      how to make rainbows
in straw hats by close-up squinting.

      To have this afternoon,
squiffy and forgiving,
      willow fronds

and boats singing off rowdily
      down the river
out of sight.

      If she couldn't make something of that
where would she be
      come the downpour?

I DO

Despite having broken the same promise
over and over. Despite knowing my failure
of the last ten years to not want other men
and to not do something about it.

Despite this being a good start but not everything.
Not enough for my one life. Despite knowing
I will continue to need to believe I could step aside
from this and run off to the Norwegian wilderness.

Forgive me my weaknesses. I'll forgive you
your alternative weaknesses—your snideness
from the sofa at home during my
disappearances. Your condescension.

Despite this and more like this, I'll put my hand
in yours in front of a churchful of witnesses.
Promise you anything, anything, my tender
and erring and uncertain darling, that you want.

Forever and ever.
Champagne.

TWO DEATH IN THE AFTERNOONS, PLEASE

Dad, now you're dead you scare me.
Every time I think about stepping into traffic
I think of you building your glass castle,
cornershop-whisky-bottle by cornershop-whisky-bottle.

I had to do one of those questionnaires recently:
How many times in the last month has your drinking
stopped you doing things you needed or wanted to do?
I put *zero*, Dad—proud nothing. They never ask

about the times the drink makes living possible.
I think of your kitchen-drinking nights, how you told me
you didn't get hangovers anymore
and I was too young to reply.

When I'm scared, Dad, I know a gluey-gold inch
of brandy, or one gin and tonic's scouring effervescence,
will lift me to arm's-length from caring, will calm me
in a bubble of slight incapacity.

The old dread, Dad—I think now you carried it
like a wolf in your stomach.
The drink quiets it, but it doesn't drown.
I recently learned another cocktail by Hemingway—

Death in the afternoon, champagne and absinthe.
You'd find the name as funny as I do.
He recommended three or five in slow succession.
When I make them, I toast him. He's family.

Dad, you're nothing now.
It's only the thought of your life that scares me.
But if there were an afterlife I'd meet you there, happy hour.
It'd be dimlit and we'd sit low in a booth and they'd keep

bringing the drinks in fine heavy glasses
and no one would interrupt to say this wasn't actually heaven,
this delicious blunting of feeling, this merciful cessation,
and that there was something outside that was better—

like walking out on the seafront together, wind and water-roar
and saying something risky and being understood.

MES BRAVES

O girls who go out in the night without coats,
without tights, in the year-round rain—I salute
your hazelnut navels, your peep-toe boots,
your goose-pimpled impudence.

Let the old-at-heart sneer! Their loss—if a glimpse
of you in the sleet doesn't light up their night.
It's freezing wet and for you it is June.
You make a mirrorball out of the rain.

OLD MAN FALLEN DOWN IN THE PUB,

well might you smile. Helped up
by strangers, you know your postcode
and they call you a taxi.

Whatever else you say
has the cadences of human speech
but we can't get a word of it.

You are far from everything that hurts
and keep smiling to avoid a beating.
You look like the future.

I speak loudly, slowly, carefully
down into your hopeful face. As if
we didn't understand each other perfectly.

From the door I look back
and you're smiling, not daring to lift
the glass of water the barman's brought you.

HE'S IN HIS ALTITUDES

The sun's in his eyes.
He's sniffed the barmaid's apron.
He's been bitten by the tavern bitch.
He's on a date with John Barleycorn.
He's got a piece of bread and cheese in the attic.
He's a couple of chapters into the novel.
He's all mops and brooms.
He's moist around the edges.
He's iced to the eyebrows.
His teeth have caught cold.
He's lit up like a church window.
His breath's strong enough to carry coal.
He's bowing to the bottle.
He's bearing his blushing honours thick upon him.
It's starlight with him.
He's among the philistines.
He's been to Olympus and now he's in Liquor Pond.
He's blind as a boiled owl, his head full of bees.
He's sober as a judge on a Friday.
He's bar-kissing.
He's lapping in the gutter.
He's laughing at the carpet.
He's keeping his sails up, beating on against an ale-head wind.
He's swallowed a hare.
He's keg-legged.
There's a brick in his hat.
He's Adam's apple up.
He's in bed with his boots on.

PLAYING THE HARP HOME

'To play the harp home'—to drunkenly make your way home by the railings

He plays the harp each Saturday night,
fades and brightens, streetlight to streetlight,
along the city's railings, holding tight
to the fifty-year-old iron. Never quite
barred, never quite forgiven. The White
Horse, The Ten Bells, The Last, The Knight
at Arms. After hours, the evening kites
through his head: the rounds, the songs, the spite
in the barmaid's voice: No more tonight.
Home along the harp-strings, he plays delight.

NOT NEVER

Don't tell me what happened. Don't say gin.
Let me lie in my lovely loss and look in
on hours I didn't exist. Leave me be:
newborn, untainted. It wasn't me.

Never another night leaving no trace?
Thanks be to the goddess who had the grace
to safe-stagger me home, insensible, wipe
away any me that was out there last night.

You can list all you like all the shots down the bar.
You may have been there. Not me. Not never.
A blank magic took me. I don't want to know
what zombie stayed, how low she'd go.

Never tequila? Never again?
Don't tell me: main drag, one-heeled, rain?
Not the morning lightning. Not the refrain
(just like last time), *Never again.*

HE PRETENDS HE DOESN'T KNOW
THE WAY TO THE STATION

Gorgeous. Inappropriate. He keeps stride
till I work the talk around to my boyfriend,
then he peels away like a shark, wishing me
every happiness. I check my pockets
all the way home—I can't work out
what I'm missing. Until I realise that this
is another of my escape poems.

I still see him cruising the shoals of commuters,
silver-beautiful as a trick of the light.
I never looked at him full on. It reminds me
of those stories where you go under the hill
with the King of the Faeries and dance
till everyone's dead. Back and forth
on the 7.40, the 17.02.

THE GROWING-CYCLE OF THE PLASTIC DAFFODIL

I'm settled now. Each spring, I know,
the house across from the shop
puts out its plastic daffs
on the table in its bay

and long ago and far away
my dead dad sneaks out overnight
to plant a plastic yellow bunch
of fakes amongst his lover's flowerbeds
(before she dies, this is)—a tease
that takes her in, almost to August.

This is the way the seasons go.
The way someone unseen puts out
a weird and plastic tribute. Out of love,
we have to hope.

ACKNOWLEDGMENTS:

Gratitude is expressed to the editors of the following magazines
in which some of these poems were first published: *Lighthouse,
Magma, Poetry News, The Interpreter's House, The North, The Rialto*.
'Ship in a Bottle' was first included in the
Templar Press anthology of poems, Mill, 2015

Thanks also to Norwich Stanza (especially Julia Webb, Richard
Lambert, Heidi Williamson, Esther Morgan, Peter Wallis and
Sally Festing); Moniza Alvi and her Poetry School seminar group
(especially Laura Scott, Stuart Charlesworth, Pippa Chapman
and Nicola Warwick); Anna Reckin and her Saturday Writers
group (especially Anne Osbourn, Lynn Woollacott, Dot Cobley
and Nedra Westwater); the Café Writers committee and all our
regulars. Also everyone on the Poetry Trust Advanced Seminar
2011; the Poetry Business Writing School 2017; and the Arvon
and Poetry School courses and tutors, especially Michael Laskey,
Ann and Peter Sansom, Mimi Khalvati, Daljit Nagra, Cliff Yates,
Helen Mort, Catherine Smith and Melissa Lee-Houghton.

And finally special appreciation to my toxic friends, cocktail
compadres, drinking buddies and hangover companions:
especially Adam, Claire, Robert, Ida and the BBO team.